A MONOGRAPHIC

IVANKA VASENSKA
ANI STOYKOVA
MARIYA PASKALEVA

SMART ANALYSIS OF TOURISM POLICY EFFICIENCY IN BULGARIA FOR THE PERIOD 1980-2017

ISBN: 978-83-957713-9-2
https://doi.org/10.2478/9788395793806

2020

Abstract: *The purpose of this study is to determine the role of tourism in the economy of Bulgaria. In this paper, we present the history of the Bulgarian tourism industry trends from the beginning to its contemporary policy patterns. We apply an econometric methodology consisting of unit root test, cointegration analysis, linear regression, correlation analysis, Granger causality test and 3-D visualizations by IBM Watson Studio based on the statistics for the period 1980-2017. Exploring the link between tourism and the economic development of Bulgaria, the tourism – led - growth hypothesis about Bulgaria is validated for the post-communism period. Our findings show that a relationship between tourism and Bulgaria's economic development exists. We can conclude that tourism is in part an endogenous growth process.*

Key words: *tourism development, economic growth, Granger causality test, co-integration, 3- D visualizations, Tourism-Led Growth Hypothesis, Bulgaria.*

3

Contents

INTRODUCTION 5

CHAPTER ONE: The history of the Bulgarian tourism industry and its trends 9

CHAPTER TWO: EMPIRICAL COMPARISON OF BULGARIAN TOURISM FOR THE PERIOD 1980-2017 27

2.1. Studies on the relationship between tourism development and the economic growth 27

2.2. Data and methodology 40

2.2.1. Data and descriptive statistics 40

2.2.2. Panel Unit Root Test: Summary 46

2.2.3. Correlation 46

2.2.4. Granger Causality 47

2.2.5. Linear Regression 48

2.2.6. Cointegration test 49

2.2.7. 3-D visualization 50

2.3. Empirical results 51

2.3.1. Empirical results for the first period 1980-1989 ... 51

2.3.2. Empirical results for the second period 1990 - 2017 58

CONCLUSION 70

REFERENCES 73

Appendix 1. 81

Appendix 2. 82

https://doi.org/10.2478/9788395793806-001

INTRODUCTION

It all changed for the people in the People's Republic of Bulgaria on November 10, 1989. During the evening central news emission on Bulgarian State Television the stepping down of power of the communist party leader was announced as unanimously decision of the Party upper-crust. The economy and power shift in every social and economic sphere started then but it hasn't finished just yet. For the one and only hotel chain in Bulgaria - "Interhotels - Balkantourist" was the beginning of the end. During the period from 1944 till 1989 the so-called tourism sector then was one of few economic activities bringing foreign currency flows in to the Bulgarian economy, respectively in the state budged and vaults of the Bulgarian National Bank.

As it outlined below, especially during the Communism period, the state governance and policy for strategic development of the tourism sector were strongly influenced by private economic interest which successfully managed to sabotage all good-intended and well planes sector development plans and strategies. Moreover, such development plans and strategies disruptions succeeded to deeply influence the synchrony on the tourism operating systems on all levels.

5

At the modern stage of its development, tourism has been influenced by numerous technical innovations. Satellite links facilitate communication and enhance interest in remote countries and areas, thus stimulating the development of international tourism. Global computer information systems (especially the wold wide web) have a multifaceted application and change the traditional ways of booking, posting, supply and market positioning. The commercialization of air transport, which began in the late 1950s, makes it possible to tour around the American, African and Australian markets by tour operators and tourists from Europe and Asia respectively.

Nowadays, we are witnesses of trends shifting by the minute and several economic, social, natural and several terrorist cataclysms later, academics and research circles are forced to employ unconventional multidisciplinary tools in order to forecast better, analyse even better and try to pull a brave face when all the scientific mumbo jumbo is offset by the whim of destiny.

The purpose of this study is to determine the role of tourism in the economy of Bulgaria. In this paper, we present the history of the Bulgarian tourism industry trends from the communism to its contemporary policy patterns aiming at establishing probable repeated patterns. We aim to explore the relationship between tourism industry and economic growth in

Bulgaria from two perspectives. First, we explore the influence of tourism on economic growth during post-communism period. This may be considered as an ex-post analysis in the sense that it includes the policies during democracy in recent years. We apply an econometric methodology consisting of unit root test, cointegration analysis, linear regression, correlation analysis and Granger causality test based on the statistics for the period 1980-2017. Exploring the link between tourism and the economic development of Bulgaria, the tourism – led - growth hypothesis about Bulgaria is validated for the capitalism period. Our findings show that a relationship between tourism and Bulgaria's economic development exists for the period from 1990 to 2017.

Restrictive conditions of this research are determined in the following aspects:

Time range - this research is restricted in the time interval from 1980- 2017;

Methodological restrictions –they are set by the statistical properties of the researched data imposing the application of specific econometric tests and models giving opportunity for the reflection. The proposed and used methodology does not claim to be the only possible and applicable when inspecting and proving the research thesis of this study;

Place restrictions – the analysis and the inspection of the research thesis are concentrated on one country - Bulgaria.

https://doi.org/10.2478/9788395793806-002

CHAPTER ONE: The history of the Bulgarian tourism industry and its trends

In the current study we intend to elaborate the history of the Bulgarian tourism industry trends from its early industrialization till its contemporary policy making. Furthermore, our aim is to compare and if possible, to establish the policies patterns – the pre-ottoman period, the periods between the two World Wars following the communist-socialist one and the transitional-contemporary one. The methodology will be based on analytical and empirical apparatus constructed on all available and achieved data. Sort of speak we will try to be masters of our own destiny without crossing the line of objectivity.

Traditions can be found from the time of the Thracians, who built near the warm "healing" spring's nymphuriums - sanctuaries dedicated to the river nymphs. Later, the Greeks built their settlements and asclepions, and later the Romans improved them building healing centres based on "sanum per aqua". Town settlements like Sofia, Burgas, Kustendil, Bankia, Hisaria and Varna were established during the antiquity by natural mineral springs.

Bulgaria is at the crossroads of the Balkan Peninsula and a number of travellers have visited it for scientific, commercial and other purposes. There are also data from the Middle Ages about the treatment of the Byzantine and Roman princes in the numerous mineral settlements and balneological regions of Bulgaria. Much of these trips are also related to frequent wars, crusades and other military movements.

Until the Liberation of Ottoman rule (1878), tourism in Bulgaria made its first steps. Tourist character had visits that the population of the surrounding villages made to the thermal mineral springs and the primitive baths (Ilagi) built around them for the purpose of treating or satisfying hygienic needs. The monasteries were other attractive places for visits by the Bulgarian population. There were thousands of people going on holidays during the holidays. The monasteries had shelters for the pilgrims. The Turkish population headed similar trips to mosques and graves of Turkish saints (tequette). Many people have been attracted by periodic collections, markets and fairs where various goods have been exhibited and sold.

All of these travels in shape have the characteristic features of tourism. In essence, however, they are very primitive and correspond to the socio-economic conditions that existed in the then Ottoman Empire. Compared with the development of tourism in Western European countries, at that time it is completely behind in our country.

Following the Liberation in 1891, the "Hot and Cold Waters Act in the Principality of Bulgaria" was adopted - one of the oldest in Europe **(Йорданов & Алексова, 2013)**. In the first years after the Liberation, the population of the Principality of Bulgaria was just over 2 million. Then the picture was quite different from today - more than 80% of the population lived in the villages and the largest Bulgarian cities were with a population of 20,000 to 30,000 people. After the Unification in 1885, the population grew to over 3 million - 3 154 375 inhabitants. According to the population census of 1888, the biggest Bulgarian city was Plovdiv. Important institutions are concentrated in the city and in 1888 there is a population of 33,032 people. Sofia, when it became a capital in 1879, was a population of nearly 12,000 people. Only 9 years later, the city increased its inhabitants to 30,428. The third largest city was Rousse, with a population of 27,194 people, due to its development during the Ottoman domination, when it was the capital of the Danube Vilayet, a large area stretching in today's northern Bulgaria. In the 19th century, Rousse was called "Little Vienna". Its favourable location on the Danube leads to its turbulent development and the introduction of a number of innovations for the first time right there. Varna was the fourth largest city with a population of 25 256 people. Its location on the Black Sea leads to rapid commercial and industrial development. It is an interesting fact that at the time of the Liberation, the Bulgarians in the town were a minority - only 3,500 people in the 20,000 population, but in the following years many Bulgarians settled in the town.

For the period from the Liberation until the First World War (1878-1918) can be related to the previous one, the restoration of Bulgarian statehood, the development of crafts, the industry and other branches of the economy. Numerous inns, hotels, restaurants, especially in the period 1900-1912, were emerging. The pebble of the "pearl of the Black Sea" also attracted the ruling elite. In 1882 prince (knyaz) Alexander Batenberg ordered that the palace Euxinograd, which served as his summer residence. Unfortunately, the trips of foreigners in Bulgaria are very limited by the Balkan, Inter-Allied wars, the First World War. By its very nature, the development of tourism in the first years after the Liberation and the wars retains some of the tokens of the early liberation period. Changes in the socio-economic conditions in the liberated Bulgarian state brought new features to tourism. Manifestation of balneological tourism was taking place. Many new thermal baths were being built near many in the vicinity of numerous thermal springs and many well-known bathing places (Hissar, Varshets, Kostenets, Ladzhene, Chepino, Kyustendil and others). The number of pilgrims in the big and famous monasteries (Rilski, Bachkovski, Troyanski, Preobrazhenski and others) was increasing. Local conferences and fairs attracted many more visitors. The city of Varna was transformed into real resort only after the First World War. The official Municipality establishing statement is dated 10 June 1921 and a week later the first bating suites season was open. Sooner rather than later without being leading for the local economy recreational sea and balneological tourism had begun to attract more and more visitors **(Иванова, 2018).** Varna's tourism superstructure was developed with fast paste and by the mid 30's the town had a casino, twenty odd hotels, vast number restaurants and liquor establishments in which orchestras performed fashionable melodies. The hotels and the private lodgings were categorized and the standards were observed by the Municipality. According to the official data, during the summer the resort populate with 70 000 residents was visited by nearly 20 000 predominantly inbound tourists as international tourists were mainly Czechs, Slovaks, Poles and Romanians and rarely French. Germans, Austrians totalling up to 5-6 000 **(Иванова, 2018).**

The next pivotal moment in Bulgarian tourism development worth mentioning is the establishment of travel bureau "Balkan" at General Directorate of Railways and Ports in 1937. The bureau had covenant relationships with most

European travel agencies, organized inbound tours and outbound travels and sold tickets domestic and international travels **(Иванова, 2018).** Two years following its establishment the bureau founded specialised department responsible for the international tourism, destination Bulgaria's promotion, publication of tourist advertising material and their distribution to travel stations and ports.

After the communist party came into power, Bulgaria carried out the nationalization of private enterprises and agricultural lands, which left them unable to pay much of their international debt. Georgi Dimitrov (Bulgarian head of state and leader of the Bulgarian Communists Party and the post-World War II prime minister (1946-1949) and the Czechoslovak head of state developed a unique solution by allowing Czechoslovak tourists to vacation on the Black Sea coast as a form of a barter style payment (Pickles, 2008, p.176). The first Bulgarian tour operator and tour agent, Balkantourist (still in operation) was established on January 6, 1948 (**Маринова, 2017**) (although its existence can be found in the guidebooks of 1939). The greatest prospect of development, of course, was the Black Sea, as the foundations of tourism had been laid for such an activity.

Soon after this, on January 6, 1948, Balkantourist was established **(Маринова, 2017).** For its activity, the state is relinquishing a number of hotels in the big Bulgarian cities. The greatest prospect of development, of course, is the Black Sea. Moreover, the foundations of tourism there have long been laid. The sea capital - Varna attracts holidaymakers for years, there is the resort of St. St Konstantin and Elena.

The necessity of a new hotel on the Black Sea coast appeared in 1948, as according to the treaty with Czechoslovakia the same year in the city of Varna began to arrive tourists. Due to the lack of a large, comfortable hotel, they are accommodated in private accommodation.

At the end of the year the construction of the new hotel "Roza", whose location was decided to be near the monastery "St. St. Konstantin and Elena"? With fierce and hard work, the building was completed and put into operation until the next tourist season - the summer of 1949.

On the beach of the hotel "Rose" were introduced for the first time the umbrellas - made especially by the Varna shipyard. Even when it was opened, however, it was clear that the hotel would not be able to accommodate the many tourists. It is necessary to build another building. This is the new Odessos Hotel, whose creation was decided in 1950. In order to be ready for the summer of 1951, Czechoslovak holidaymakers also took part in the construction activity. The second and a half of the third floor of Odessos are entirely built by Czech tourists.

In 1955 the real expansion of the resort, called at that time "Varna", and later - Druzhba began. A number of hotels, restaurants, sports facilities, etc. were built. Of course, there is also a place to relax for important guests. This is Chaika Hotel, which hosts Bulgarian and foreign rulers, world famous actors, singers and so on. The frequent guests are famous Bulgarian celebrities Lamar, Mr. Senko and others.

Interestingly enough, at that time it was not considered mandatory for each hotel room to have a bathroom. For this reason, only the rooms at Chaika Hotel, which looked out over the sea, were equipped with a shower room and a sink, and the rest of them had only a sink.

Foreign tourist companies are also interested in the Bulgarian resort. Among them, Druzhba became known as the "Red Riviera" - because of the Communist government of the country. There is not much entertainment in the complex. Therefore, for the holiday makers, excursions are organized by carriages to the nearby Uzunkum - Long Sand beach, where the Golden Sands Resort is currently located. Then the place is wild and quite populated with snakes.

Soon, however, carts cease to work. There is a need to invent new means of transport. A group of the Swedish

Communist Party arrives at the Roza Hotel with a new Scania bus, at the invitation of Bulgarian comrades. The Swedes are staying here for 15 days, and when their departure time comes, they offer for a further 10 days a free stay and a train to Sweden to donate the resort's bus. The proposal was initially rejected by the rulers in Sofia, but after a brief reflection on their part, the idea was approved. Thus, Varna acquires a new "Scania", which becomes an attraction for most residents of our sea capital.

By the middle of the decade there is the long-awaited change in the tourist flow, which was originally Soviet, Czechoslovak, Polish and Hungarian guests. Western tourists with a predominant number of FGDs appear. All of a sudden, the idea to build a big Bulgarian Black Sea resort was born. For this purpose, the area "Uzunkum", which combines a wild forest and a beautiful beach, was chosen. In 1956 the first new international resort Golden Sands was made.

However, a serious problem emerges from the builders - the snakes. The area is literally a hangout of dozens of reptile's nests. Zoo specialists had to step in and walk around with snakes in naked hands. However, they did not manage to eliminate all the animals - new and new rounds of reptiles emerged in the construction process. Here comes the nature itself. It has long been known that the natural enemy of the snakes are hedgehogs. That's why 200-300 barbed-up creatures were imported specially from Albania and released around the area. Soon there were no reptiles on the beach.

It is interesting to mention that before the Golden Sands was built, there was a lake in the area inhabited by water turtles. According to the idea of the architects at that time, however, one of the most prestigious hotels - "International" - was built on it. For this purpose, in the basement of the building were built pumps that constantly suck out the water from the lake. Gradually, dozens of hotels were built, while in 1966 the final stage of construction was completed. With this endeavour, the big international tourism in our country is being started.

As early as 1957 a decision was taken to build a second similar complex on the Bulgarian Black Sea coast. This time, the beach north of Nessebar was chosen for this place. At that time the area was not particularly loved by Nessebar people. However, a commission specifically designated for this purpose finds that there is the most favourable conditions for sea and sea treatment from all of our southern coast. This is where Ferdinand wanted to build a second Euxinograde. Thus, begins the history of the largest Bulgarian Black Sea resort Sunny Beach. And the prospect was to build the entire bay between Cape Emine and the town of Sozopol.

At that time, however, it turned out that just where they wanted to build, an international student camp was located, attended mainly by students from Poland and the GDR. The state describes the property of the settlement, compensates it with 79 million leva and gives it a new place south of Primorsko. The camp is built again. Subsequently, it grew and developed by launching the current International Youth Center (IYC).

The original construction concept of Sunny Beach, as well as Golden Sands, was the buildings to be no higher than three floors. When the construction of the 10-storey "Astoria" in Golden Sands in 1960 began, it turned out that the taller buildings were more suitable.

In the late 1960s, our third big sea resort - Albena appeared. In its place is chosen the coast between the village of Kranevo and the Rusalka (The Fish) resort. At that time Kranevo was a declining settlement and even had an idea to be deleted from the map of Bulgaria. However, with the construction of the large complex nearby, the village was reborn for a new life. Albena surpassed other resorts with tourist and commercial services, attraction and entertainment cabaret programs in the theme restaurants, bazaar centres, excellent conditions and facilities for all kinds of water sports and most of all with care for children.

The popularity of the resort was due to the wonderful surroundings, old settlements and new recreation centers: Balchik, Tuzlata, Kavarna and the cultural and historical remains of Kaliakra and Tauk liman, the gulf where the resort Rusalka grew, reminding of the unique panorama of Veliko Tarnovo with the white one-storey buildings, hanging on the rocks. Rusalka, was designed and built by a Mediterranean style club model and it was one of the most attractive places in Europe for recreation and entertainment. The glory of the resort grows very quickly - in 1969 the "1 million tourist" was registered, in 1973 - the "two million". This popularity was also due to the three major international music events united in the festival "Holidays of Sunny Beach" - the International Golden Orpheus Song Festival, the International Folklore Festival and the Decade of Symphonic Music.

As early as the 1970s, the country had the number of hotels is 40, the beds are 12 850, the camps are three with 7500 beds, restaurants - 22 with 13 300 seats **(Иванов, 2014)** and the ten million tourists limit was passed, but continues to assimilate the sea strip partly to the north and mainly to the south. By 1974, the main stage of the development of the Bulgarian Riviera was build and operations were in progress. Its popularity was also due to the three major international music events united in the festival "Holidays of Sunny Beach"

- the International Golden Orpheus Song Festival, the International Folklore Festival and the Decade of Symphonic Music **(Иванов, 2014).**

Tourism advertising, which largely depends on the success of the industry abroad, is carried out by the Balkantourist offices abroad. The international tourist fairs in Berlin, Moscow, Madrid, Milan, Paris, Gothenburg and elsewhere, where Bulgarian pavilions attract many visitors, play a significant role in the development of tourism. The international entertainment events, such as racing competition Golden Sands (Rali Zlatni Pyasatsi) and the Golden Orpheus Competition were of great importance **(Маринова, 2017).**

According to Ivanova (2018), the Politburo adopted in 1960 by the Political Bureau of the Central Committee of the Bulgarian Communist Party (BKP) initiate ambitious plans for a large-scale investment program for construction of new infrastructure, increase of the bed numbers and superstructure, reconstruction of cultural and historical monument, developing of different types of tourism (besides sea tourism). Investing in mountain and balneological destination was already on the agenda. The investments were directed not only to the Black Sea coast and into smaller towns with already established traditions in tourism, namely Bankya, Hisar, Varshets, Borovets. Investment intentions in entirely new resorts have also been pledged - Pamporovo, Vasil Kolarov Dam (today - Golyam Beglik), national sites have been established - Pirin Mountain, the Danube River and some of the big caves, the archaeological exploration of the old Bulgarian capitals was resumed - Pliska (681 to 893), Preslav (893 to 971), Vliko Tarnovo (1185 to 1396 and 1878-1879). Unfortunately, the only tangible result of this ambitious program was the construction of the Pamporovo ski resort and the development of the Borovets resort. The alternative destinations to maritime tourism remained empty, more over the interest in the Black Sea increasied. All attempts to attract segments of the socialist bloc, for balneotherapy and rehabilitation in Hissar failed. Although winter ski tourism meet the competition of the already established winter resorts of the former Eastern Bloc, it attracted a significant number of tourists but beginan to generate and loss. Then Balkantourist began to redirect tourists from the Black Sea coast for one and two-day trips inland. There were two goals: the international tourists to get acquainted with the rich cultural, historical and natural heritage of Bulgaria and to "illustrate the benefits of the socialist system" **(Ivanova, 2018).** The first foreign advertisements of Kazanlak and the Valley of the Roses, Plovdiv and the Rila Monastery date the mid-1960s, which brought them international popularity and earned them recognition as new symbols of Bulgarian tourism. During this period, the BCP commenced to appreciate foreign exchange earnings from international tourism, which were increased as a result of the improved quality of the offered tourism product.

A natural change began in the Bulgarian tourist product supply strategy goals - from extensive and mass to elite and intensive without any ordering, monitoring and sanctioning by the BCP. Unfortunately, the currency crisis started in 1976-1977 and concentrated the attention of the political elite which with Decision No. 481redefined the main strategic objective of the sector - "to increase the efficiency of international business tourism and to bring the industry to one of the foremost places for providing foreign exchange revenue" **(Ivanova, 2018).** The aim was to implement all types of tourism - balneological and spa, mountain, cultural, business, etc., modernizing and reconstructuring the available facilities in order to develop luxury and to increase foreign exchange earnings.

The last conceptual discussion of international tourism political strategy in the Politburo was in 1987 **(Ivanova, 2018),** in which was old song to a new tune, but a significant diversification of the tourism product supply, extension of the season and the lack of a strategy allowed external according to Ivanova **(Ivanova, 2018)** "responsible factors" in the Party hierarchy to interfere and according to an internal analysis done by Balkantourist in 1984, the enterprise backlog is mainly due to party-motivated investments made without market-oriented research of supply and calculation of profitability.

Undoubted successes in tourism, however, are accompanied by a number of mistakes in the construction of the base and in the service, which together form the series of unresolved problems in the economic tourism until 1989. The richest individual tourists, who cannot get luxury amenities against their money, were repelled.

However, throughout the socialist period tourism was a very profitable economic sector, providing the convertible international currency needed for the development of the economy and the social sector. Its contribution has increased multiplied due to the opportunities it provided especially for pupils, students and children for camping at sea and mountain at affordable prices.

The construction of the so-called Southern Black Sea Complex, which includes Primorsko, is planned under the design of Balkantourist south of Sozopol. This project is never implemented, but the site is covered by the campsite network and resort villages. In 1987, Bulgaria has 98 campsites, which have 14 165 beds in bungalows and 65 000 places for camping. Among the villages, called holiday homes, two win international recognition - one is Duni, south of Sozopol, the other is Elenite, to the north of Sunny Beach. With their unique and inimitable style, they welcome their first guests in the late 1980s.

Undoubted successes in tourism, however, were accompanied by a number of missteps in the construction of the accommodation base and in the service, which together form the series of unresolved issues in tourism until 1989. The richest individual tourists, who cannot get luxury amenities against their money, were repelled. However, tourism throughout the socialist period was a very profitable sector, providing the hard currency needed for the development of the economy and the social sector. Its contribution has increased many times and due to the opportunities, it provided for millions of people, pupils, students and children for recreation by sea coast and mountainous regions at affordable prices.

Following 10 November 1989 and the fall of the Berlin wall, Bulgaria's tourism industry has been object to large amount of uncertainties. Touristic flows within the ex-USSR and Eastern bloc were crucially shifted and tourism demand and supply for this region dramatically declined for particular period. Furthermore, political power shifts within Bulgaria led to a period of stagnation and then to a program of political and economic reform which, while increasing in momentum has left the bulk of state assets including those in tourism, in state hands **(Harrison, 1993)**. According to Ivanov **(Ivanov, 2017)**, during the 1990s, Bulgaria began to move to a market orientated economy moreover the rough transition deeply disturbed the established distribution channels and drown touristic flows. The sharp decline in the flows from Central and Eastern European countries, which were facing similar political, economic and social changes **(Bachvarov, 1997 and Harrison, 1993 cited by Ivanov, 2017)**, was the conductor of fall in number of tourists and accommodation establishments for the period 1990-1992 **(Ivanov, 2017)**. The statistic renders an account plummeted number of beds - from 303,912 in 1990 to just 117,740 in 1999, while international arrivals declined from 10.3 million in 1990 to 5.06 million in 1999 (National Statistics Institute [NSI], 2001 cited by **Ivanov, 2017**). The 1990s were the beginning of tourism industry was completely liberalisation and the most of hotels and resorts were privatised, and "currently the sector is nearly 100% private" **(Ivanov, 2017)**. Much in this vein, it should be noted that a lot of efforts have been made in the training of the tourism professionals, prepared to meet the touristic service demand in the new establishments. As a positive feature can me mentioned is the transition from hard to soft skills **(Kriyakova-Dineva, Kyurova & Chankova, 2019)**.

https://doi.org/10.2478/9788395793806-003

CHAPTER TWO: EMPIRICAL COMPARISON OF BULGARIAN TOURISM FOR THE PERIOD 1980-2017

2.1. Studies on the relationship between tourism development and the economic growth

The positive effects of tourism development on the economic growth have fostered the emergence of the tourism-led growth (TLG) hypothesis **(Balaguer and Cantavella-Jordá, 2002).** According to this hypothesis, tourism expansion increases the long - run economic growth. Additionally, the development of the tourism sector has usually been viewed as a positive contribution to economic growth. A large number of studies have examined the tourism-led growth hypothesis. The results of these studies have been mixed and inconsistent. Many studies support the TLG hypothesis **(Brida et al., 2008; Gunduz and Hatemi-J, 2005; Nowak and Sahli, 2007; Tang and Abosedra, 2016; Tang and Tan, 2015).** However, a number of studies have identified the reverse effect, that economic development boosts tourism expansion **(Lee, 2012; Oh, 2005; Payne and Mervar, 2010; Tang and Jang, 2009).** Many researchers conclude that the TLG hypothesis may be country specific **(Lee and Chang, 2008; Holzner, 2011).**

Dimitrov et al. (2018) prove that there is a strong association, a strong correlation between levels of GDP of the concerned EU-countries and the number of foreign visitors to Bulgaria with recreation and holiday aims. This strong association also indicates one of the weaknesses of the Bulgarian tourism industry, and namely that it relies to a great extent on low-income and low-price customers **(Dimitrov et al., 2018).**

Shan and Wilson (2001) propose Tourism led Growth (TLG) hypothesis and their findings indicate that trade flows do link with tourism in the case of China. Empirical evidence that aims to identify tourism-growth relationship behaviour are presented in various empirical researches. **Singh (2008)** examines a link between tourism and economic development among 37 small developing islands and proves the existence of such linkages. This study applied simple cross-sectional regression model to estimate the relationship between economic development and tourism receipts, additionally, tourism income multipliers estimated for several of the islands. According to **Brida et al (2014)** tourism as a significant employment generator increases and activates income for residents through multiplier effects. **Salahodjaev and Safarova (2015)** provide empirical evidence that tourism exerts a positive and significant effect on economic growth after controlling for conventional determinants in the growth equation in 23 post-communist countries, including Bulgaria for the period 1990-2012.

Surugiu and Surugiu (2013) use the cointegration method and Granger causality analysis based on the vector error correction model (VECM) and impulse functions in order to examine the long-run relationships between tourism expansion and economic growth in Romania during the period 1988-2009. They find that there are Granger causality relationships running from tourism expansion to economic growth, which sustains the tourism-led growth hypothesis (TLGH). **Chou (2013)** examines causal relationships between tourism spending and economic growth in 10 countries in Central and Eastern Europe for the period 1988–2011. The author concludes that for 3 of these 10 countries (Bulgaria, Romania and Slovenia), the neutrality hypothesis is in the nature of a causal direction between tourism spending and economic growth. **Aslan (2013)** studies the relationship between tourism development and economic growth in the Mediterranean countries using the newly developed panel Granger causality tests for the 1995–2010 period. He concludes that the growth-led tourism hypothesis is supported in case of Spain, Italy, Tunisia, Cyprus, Croatia, Bulgaria and Greece.

According to **Coşkun and Özer (2014)** tourism is an important source of economic growth, especially for developing countries. They test the tourism-led growth hypothesis in Turkey over the period 1992: Q1-2014 Q1. Their basic findings support the reciprocal casual hypothesis. They prove that tourism expansion and economic growth cause effects on each other. The relationship between them is bidirectional and economic growth may be improved by strategic planning of the tourism industry and vice versa.

Harrison (1993) confirms that since November 1989, Bulgaria's tourism industry has been faced to severe stress. According to this research the political change in Bulgaria led to a period of stalemate and after that to a program of a political and economic reform.

Deng and Ma (2014) observe that tourism activity negatively affected Chinese economic growth, principally because of weak institutions, price volatility and the crowding out of human capital. **Deng et al. (2014)** also reach the same conclusions. **Chen and Chiou-Wei (2009)** show that the tourism-led economic growth hypothesis was supported for Taiwan with a reciprocal causal relationship found for South Korea.

Ridderstaat et al. (2013) investigate the relationship between tourism development and economic growth in Aruba.

The results show there is one cointegrating relation between these two concepts, while the VECM consisted of both short and long-run relations. Their findings show that tourism is in part an endogenous growth process, and verified the presence of the TLGH in the case of Aruba.

Bento (2016) uses a disaggregated measure of tourism activity to provide additional information about the effects of domestic tourism and foreign tourism on economic growth. The results from the cointegration and causality tests support the view that the tourism-led growth hypothesis is valid for the Portuguese economy. The findings show that there is a causal link between tourism and economic growth. **Bento (2016)** proves that tourism does really matter for economic growth in Portugal.

Demirhan (2016) test the tourism-led growth hypothesis in Mediterranean countries for 1995-2013. In this study, it is proved that tourism receipts and tourism arrivals have a positive effect on economic growth in the long-run. Furthermore, the results on individual effects reveal that tourism arrivals and receipts contribute to economic growth in Bulgaria, Croatia, France, Israel, Italy, Macedonia and Portugal. The empirical results in the study prove that the tourist-led growth hypothesis.

Suhel and Bashir (2018) analyse the relationship between the number of tourists, tourism investment, government tourism spending, and economic growth in South Sumatra. They use Granger causality model and simultaneous equation model to estimate the empirical model. The findings show that the number of tourists, the added value of the tourism sector, and the tourism spending of the tourism sector affect economic growth. They prove that government policy has an important role in encouraging the tourism sector development which is indicated the contribution this sector on economic growth.

Suresh and Senthilnathan (2014) examine the causal relationship between economic growth and tourism earning in Sri Lanka during 1977-2012. They employ Granger Causality tests to analyse the presence and direction of causality between economic growth and tourism earnings and cointegration test and error correction mechanism to analyse the long-term relationship between two variables. The results reveal that there is uni-directional causality between economic growth and tourism earning, where economic growth only causes to tourism earnings, not the other way around.

Meyer (2018) analyses the relationship between tourism as the dependent variable, and economic growth, exchange rate changes and political stability, as independent variables in South Africa. The examined period is from 1996 to 2017 and Meyer uses the Johansen cointegration, Vector Error Correction and Granger causality econometric models. The results indicated that there are both long and short-run relationships between the variables.

Table 1. Summary literature review

Studies on the relationship between tourism development and the economic growth				
Authors	Explored country	Sample Period	Tests Used	Results
cint ɪlaguer and ʌnuel ɪntavella-ʀdá (2002)	Spain	1975-1997	Cointegration tests	The earnings from international tourism affect positively the Spanish economic growth. The strong impact of tourist activity, according to the magnitude of the estimated parameter would reveal the existence of important long-run multiplier effects.
ɔkman ɪnduz and bdulnasser ʌtemi-J ʹ005)	Turkey	1963-2000	Leveraged bootstrap causality tests	It is found that the tourism-led growth hypothesis is supported empirically in the case of Turkey.
an-Jacques ɪowak and ʹondher ʌhli (2007)	Small island developing states (SIDS)	1990-2002	General equilibrium model	The authors prove that increased inbound tourism may lead to net welfare losses when tourism products are intensive users of coastal land.
ʹhor Foon ɪang and	Malaysia	1975-2011	Granger causality test, Cointegration test	Tourism has a positive impact on Malaysia's economic growth

33

Eu Chye Tan (2015)				both in the short-run and in long-run. All this provides empirical support for tourism-led growth hypotl in Malaysia.
Chor Foon Tang and Salah Abosedra (2016)	Lebanon	1995-2011	Granger causality with rolling regression technique, TYDL bootstrap causality approach	The tourism-led gro hypothesis is suppo empirically in the case of Lebanese economy. They find some evidences of directional Granger causa running from the real excha rate to tourism and econc growth in Lebanon
Chew Ging Lee (2012)	Singapore	1980-2007	Bounds test, Granger causality test	The results support growth tourism, tourism-led imp and export-led tou hypotheses in the short run. results also show that imp have positive effects economic growth in the l run. It is also found that tou has indirect effects on econc growth in the long run thrc import activities.
Oh (2005)	South Korea	1975-2001	Engle-Granger approach and bivariate VAR model	There is no long-term rela between tourism and econc growth. Furthermore, accorc to Granger causality test res it is understood that there unilateral causality only f

				economic growth to tourism development.
mes E. yne and adrea ervar (2010)	Croatia	2000-2008	Toda– Yamamoto long-run causality tests	The obtained results reveal positive unidirectional causality from real GDP to international tourism revenues, as well as positive unidirectional causality from real GDP to the real effective exchange rate. Thus, the results lend support for the economic-driven tourism growth hypothesis.
nun-Hung ugo Tang d oocheong hawn) Jang 009)	United States of America (USA)	1980-2005	Cointegration and Granger causality tests.	Their results show that while no long-run relationship exists between economic growth and tourism industry performance, there is a unidirectional causality running from GDP to tourism industry performance in the United States.
hien-Chiang ee and hun-Ping hang (2008)	23 OECD countries and 32 nonOECD countries	1990-2002	Panel unit root tests, Panel cointegration tests	There is solid evidence of the panel cointegration relations between tourism development and GDP in the sample countries - both OECD and nonOECD countries. The panel causality test shows that in the long run, no matter if the tourism variable is the value of international tourism real receipts per capita or the number of international tourist arrivals per capita,

				unidirectional caus relationships exist from tou growth to econe development in O countries.
Mario Holzner (2011)	134 countries	1970-2007	Growth model, Regression A4	It is found that there is no da of a Beach Disease Effect. the contrary, tourism depen countries do not face exchange rate distortion deindustrialisation but hi than average economic grc rates. Investment in phy: capital, such as for inst; transport infrastructure, complementary to investme tourism.
Jordan Shan and Ken Wilson (2001)	China	1987-1998	Granger no-causality approach developed by Toda and Yamamoto	Findings indicate a two- Granger causality betw international travel international trade and h imply that trade flows do with tourism in the case China.
Raufhon Salahodjaev and Nilufar Safarova (2015)	23 post-communis t countries	1990-2012	Conventional growth model	They find that tou development yields statistic significant effect, at the level, on economic growth ; controlling for pote endogeneity of the right han side variables.

melia rugiu and arius zvan rugiu 013)	Romania	1988-2009	Cointegration method and Granger causality analysis based on the vector error correction model (VECM) and impulse functions	The findings suggest that there are Granger causality relationships running from tourism expansion to economic growth, which sustains the tourism-led growth hypothesis (TLGH).
ing Che ou (2013)	Bulgaria, Cyprus, the Czech Republic, Estonia, Hungary, Latvia, Poland, Romania, Slovakia and Slovenia	1988-2011	Lagrange multiplier (LM) test, e standard F test, Bootstrap panel Granger causality approach	Their empirical results indicate that for 3 of these 10 countries (Bulgaria, Romania and Slovenia), the neutrality hypothesis is in the nature of a causal direction between tourism spending and economic growth. Their results also support evidence on the growth hypothesis for Cyprus, Latvia and Slovakia.
lper Aslan 013)	Mediterra nean countries	1995-2010	panel Granger causality tests	
ci Oya oşkun and ustafa Özer 014)	Turkey	1992-2014	ARCH/GARCH model, VECM Granger tests	The results of this study indicate that tourism expansion and economic growth have effects on each other, and uncertainties in economic growth affect tourism expansion in Turkey. Additionally,tourism uncertainties have significant

				effects on economic growt[...] the short run.
Taotao Deng and Mulan Ma (2014)	China	2000-2010	resource curse hypothesis approach	The empirical results show [...] physical investment and hu[...] capital are impo[...] transmission channels thrc[...] which tourism activity indire[...] exerts more positive effect[...] economic growth. The pr[...] volatility and econc[...] openness play a positive [...] small and insignificant rol[...] explaining tourism's indi[...] effect.
Taotao Deng, Mulan Ma and Jianhua Cao (2014)	China's 30 provinces	1987-2010	Resource curse hypothesis approach	The empirical results show [...] even in the non-touri[...] dependent economies there [...] possibility that the tou[...] resource curse will occur in[...] long term. Tourism reso[...] development tends to rec[...] economic growth, ma[...] through crowding out hu[...] capital.
Ching-Fu ChenSong Zan Chiou-Wei (2009)	Taiwan and South Korea	1975-2007	EGARCH-M model	The results indicate that [...] tourism-led economic gro[...] hypothesis is supported [...] Taiwan while a reciprocal ca[...] relationship is found for S[...] Korea. The significant imp[...] of uncertainty on growth are [...] identified.

rge dderstaat, bertico oes, Peter kamp 013)	Aruba	1972-2011	Unit root, Cointegration test, VECM, Granger causality test	Tourism is in part an endogenous growth process, and verified the presence of the TLGH in the case of Aruba.
ão Paulo rdeira nto (2016)	Portugal	1995-2015	Cointegration and causality analysis	The results from the cointegration and causality tests support the view that the tourism-led growth hypothesis is valid for the Portuguese economy. The findings show that there is a causal link between tourism and economic growth.
nu mirhan 016)	Mediterra nean countries	1995-2013	Panel FMOLS and panel DOLS models	Empirical findings indicate that tourism receipts and tourism arrivals affect economic growth positively in the long-run and that these results are valid as individually, which shows tourism-led growth hypothesis is valid in Mediterranean countries.
hel Suhel d Abdul ashir (2018)	South Sumatra	2000-2015	Granger causality model, Simultaneous equation model	The number of tourists, value-added of the tourism sector, and government spending of tourism sector have the significant effect on the economic growth, while, the investments of tourism sector not significant in affecting

				economic growth in S Sumatera.
Jeyapraba Suresh and Samithamby Senthilnathan (2014)	Sri Lanka	1977-2012	Granger Causality tests	The results reveal that the uni-directional caus between economic growth tourism earning, w economic growth only caus tourism earnings, not the c way around.
Meyer (2018)	South Africa	1996-2017	Johansen cointegration, Vector Error Correction, Granger causality	The results indicated that are both long and short relationships between variables.

Source: Authors' systematization

2.2. Data and methodology

2.2.1. Data and descriptive statistics

The aim of this research is to explore the relationship between tourism and economic development of Bulgaria in the period of communism and the one of post-communism. We make attempts to investigate the validity of the tourism-led-growth (TLG) hypotheses in Bulgaria. Our dataset contains annual observations at a country level over the years 1980-2017. The explored time period is divided into two sub-periods: 1980-1989- a period when communism is established; 1990-2017- a post-communism period. Data applied for Bulgaria are annual time series. The explored variables are:

> **GDP of Bulgaria:**

GDP growth measured as annual percentage growth rate of GDP at market prices based on constant local currency. The data is from World Development Indicators (WDI).

> ### GDP per capita based on purchasing power parity (PPP):

We include this variable as a lagged dependent variable as a conventional scenario to eliminate potential autocorrelation in the residual. PPP GDP is gross domestic product converted to international dollars using purchasing power parity rates.

> ### Inflation Rate and Population growth rate:

We include inflation growth rates and population growth as control variables. The data is from the World Bank.

> ### Human Development Index (HDI):

The HDI is created to emphasize that people and their capabilities should be the ultimate criteria for assessing the development of a country, not economic growth alone. The HDI can also be used to question national policy choices, asking how two countries with the same level of GNI per capita can end up with different human development outcomes. These contrasts can stimulate debate about government policy priorities. The Human Development Index (HDI) is a summary measure of average achievement in key dimensions of human development: a long and healthy life, being knowledgeable and have a decent standard of living. The annual data is from www.knoema.com and Human Development reports.

> **International Tourist Arrival (ITA):**

Adding international tourist arrivals as a variable, allows the results to be read as a relationship between an income variable and the degrees of tourism specialization and the attractiveness of economic growth of Bulgaria and the tourists inflows.

Table 2. The explored variables

Variable	Definition/Explanation	Source
GDP	Annual percentage growth rate of GDP at market prices based on constant local currency	World Development Indicatc (WDI)- https://datacatalog.worldbank.or dataset/world-development-indicators
GDP per capita based on purchasing power parity (PPP)	Gross domestic product converted to international dollars using purchasing power parity rates	World Bank website https://data.worldbank.org/
Inflation Rate	The percentage at which a currency is devalued during a period.	World Bank website https://data.worldbank.org/
Population growth rate	The average annual rate of change of population size during a	World Bank website https://data.worldbank.org/

	specified period.	
ıman ►velopment Index DI)	Summary measure of average achievement in key dimensions of human development: a long and healthy life, being knowledgeable and have a decent standard of living	Knoema Enterprise Data Solutions www.knoema.com
ternational ►urist Arrival A)	The number of visitors from abroad to Bulgaria.	Национален статистически институт, Република България https://www.nsi.bg/

ce: Authors' systematization

Table 3 provides the main descriptive statistics of the examined variables for the period of communism. The mean is positive for all of the variables. All of the time series, except the PPP GDP are negatively skewed, indicating a higher probability of large decreases in these series than increases for this period. The values of skewness indicate that the distribution is positively skewed only for the population growth rate i.e. mean is greater than median and median is greater than mode. The kurtosis exceeds the reference value of the Gaussian distribution (equal to 3) for GDP, inflation rate and population growth rate, implying that these variables are leptokurtic. We can conclude that all of the variables except the population growth are normally distributed and we cannot reject the null hypothesis of normality for the first period *(Table 3)*. According to **Traykov et al. (2018):** *"Another graphical tool with which to assess normality is plotting histogram and compared to appropriate normal density"*.

Table 3. Descriptive Statistics for the variables for the first period (1980-1989)

	HDI	GDP	INFL	POP	ITA	PPP
Mean	0.681111	3.851316	1.089704	0.019339	2750832.	6.967556
Median	0.680000	3.430306	1.345490	0.147109	2883669.	6.841000
Maximum	0.700000	10.94469	6.729684	0.333269	4141973.	8.813000
Minimum	0.660000	-3.289882	-5.389744	-1.170039	1033808.	5.113000
Std. Dev.	0.012693	3.732332	3.260647	0.463167	970086.5	1.278770
Skewness	-0.214510	-0.001593	-0.341622	-2.142414	-0.497097	0.060635
Kurtosis	2.032402	3.742480	3.485853	6.178588	2.441120	1.753558
Jarque-Bera	0.420114	0.206733	0.263578	10.67369	0.487788	0.588122
Probability	0.810538	0.901797	0.876526	0.004811	0.783571	0.745231
Sum	6.130000	34.66184	9.807334	0.174051	24757488	62.70800
Sum Sq. Dev.	0.001289	111.4424	85.05457	1.716188	7.53E+12	13.08203

Source: Authors' calculations.

Table 4 shows the descriptive statistics of the examined variables for the period after the communism. The mean is positive for all of the variables except the population growth rate. For the second period, only the time series of GDP and population growth rate are negatively skewed, indicating a higher probability of large decreases in these series than increases. Comparing the values of skewness of different variables under consideration, it is obvious that the skewness

44

of variable INFL (inflation rate) is highly positively skewed as compared to the other values. The kurtosis values of inflation rate and population growth rate are larger than the value of normal distribution (the kurtosis of the normal distribution is 3), indicating that big shocks are more likely to be present for these variables. In comparison with the previous period, for the second period the departure from normality is confirmed by the Jarque-Bera test statistics only for the inflation rate and population growth rate and we can reject the null hypothesis of normality at the 5% level for these two variables.

Table 4. Descriptive Statistics for the variables for the second period (1990-2017)

	HDI	GDP	INFL	ITA	POP	PPP
Mean	0.743214	1.501092	59.66912	4814767.	-0.809832	10468.43
Median	0.745000	2.387548	6.310049	4565000.	-0.684342	8734.318
Maximum	0.810000	7.344422	958.5032	8252000.	-0.339586	20329.34
Minimum	0.700000	-9.117377	-0.702888	2472000.	-2.170699	4754.420
Std. Dev.	0.038783	4.713617	182.4330	1653682.	0.444160	5253.733
Skewness	0.213671	-0.894389	4.519499	0.357400	-2.097597	0.433492
Kurtosis	1.574177	2.897525	22.66608	1.972226	6.374332	1.672957
Jarque-Bera	2.584859	3.745267	546.5345	1.828467	33.81674	2.931489
Probability	0.274603	0.153718	0.000000	0.400824	0.000000	0.230906
Sum	20.81000	42.03059	1670.735	1.35E+08	-22.67530	293116.1
Sum Sq. Dev.	0.040611	599.8911	898608.9	7.38E+13	5.326515	7.45E+08

Source: Authors' calculations.

2.2.2. Panel Unit Root Test: Summary

The recent literature suggests that panel- based unit root tests have higher power than unit roots tests based on individual time series. We describe the panel unit root test by the following equation:

$$y_t = p_i y_{it-1} + x_{it} \delta_i + \varepsilon_{it} \quad (1)$$

Where i=1,2…N cross- section units, which are observed over periods t=1.2…T_i; x_{it}- exogenous variables, including fixed effects or individual trends; p_i- autoregressive coefficient; ε_{it}- errors, which are assumed to be mututally independent idiosyncratic disturbance.

We may conclude that:

1. If : p_i :< 1, y_i is considered to be trend stationary;
2. If : p_i := 1, then y_i contains a unit root. The null hypothesis assumes a common unit root process.

2.2.3. Correlation

Correlation is any of a broad class of statistical relationships involving dependence, though in common usage it most often refers to the extent to which two variables have a linear relationship with each other.

The population correlation coefficient $\hat{\rho}(X,Y)$ between two random variables X and Y is defined as:

$$\hat{\rho}(X,Y) = \frac{\hat{\sigma}(X,Y)}{(\hat{\sigma}(X,X).\hat{\sigma}(Y,Y))^{1/2}} \qquad (1)$$

A correlation coefficient is a number that quantifies a type of correlation and dependence, meaning statistical relationships between two or more values in fundamental statistics.

For example, **Sapundzhi et al (2016)** in order to find relationship between sets of data derived from in vitro assay and docking results, they use Pearson's correlation, using GraphPad Prism 3.0

2.2.4. Granger Causality

To determine the direction of the causality relationship between tourism, GDP and the other control variables; if it is one-way or bidirectional, we used Granger causality test. We analyse the relationship between the explored variables using the concept of Granger- causality.

The **Granger (1969)** approach to the question of whether x causes y is to see how much of the current y can be explained by past values of y and then to see whether adding lagged values of x can improve the explanation. y is

47

said to be Granger-caused by x if x helps in the prediction of y, or equivalently if the coefficients on the lagged x's are statistically significant. Note that two-way causation is frequently the case; x Granger causes y and y Granger causes x

It is important to note that the statement "x Granger causes y" does not imply that y is the effect or the result of x. Granger causality measures precedence and information content but does not by itself indicate causality in the more common use of the term.

EViews runs bivariate regressions of the form:

$$y_t = \alpha_0 + \alpha_1 y_{t-1} + ... + \alpha_1 y_{t-1} + \beta_1 x_{t-1} + ... + \beta_1 x_{-1} + \varepsilon_t \qquad (2)$$

$$x_t = \alpha_0 + \alpha_1 x_{t-1} + ... + \alpha_1 x_{t-1} + \beta_1 y_{t-1} + ... + \beta_1 y_{-1} + u_t \qquad (3)$$

for all possible pairs of (x, y) series in the group.

2.2.5. Linear Regression

In order to reveal the direct relationship between tourism and economic growth of Bulgaria, we apply linear regression from the following type:

$$GDP = \alpha ITA + \beta \qquad (4)$$

2.2.6. Cointegration test

The finding that many macro time series may contain a unit root has spurred the development of the theory of non-stationary time series analysis. **Engle and Granger (1987)** pointed out that a linear combination of two or more non-stationary series may be stationary. If such a stationary linear combination exists, the non-stationary time series are said to be cointegrated. The stationary linear combination is called the cointegrating equation and may be interpreted as a long-run equilibrium relationship among the variables. We apply cointegration tests employing the **Johansen (1991, 1995)** system framework.

EViews supports VAR-based cointegration tests using the methodology developed in **Johansen (1991, 1995)** performed using a Group object or an estimated VAR object.

Consider a VAR of order p :

$$y_t = A_1 y_{t-1} + \cdots + A_p y_{t-p} + B x_t + \epsilon_t \qquad (5)$$

Where y_t is a k vector of non-stationary I(1) variables, x_t is a d-vector of deterministic variables, and ϵ_t is a vector of innovations. We may rewrite this VAR as,

$$\Delta y_t = \Pi y_{t-1} + \sum_{i=1}^{p-1} \Gamma_i \Delta y_{t-i} + B x_t + \epsilon_t \qquad (6)$$

where:

$$\Pi = \sum_{i=1}^{p} A_i - I, \qquad \Gamma_i = -\sum_{j=i+1}^{p} A_j$$

(7)

Granger's representation theorem asserts that if the coefficient matrix Π has reduced rank $r < k$, then there exist $k \times r$ matrices α and β each with rank r such that $\Pi = \alpha\beta'$ and $\beta' y_t$ is I(0). r is the number of cointegrating relations (*the cointegrating rank*) and each column of β is the cointegrating vector. As explained below, the elements of α are known as the adjustment parameters in the VEC model. Johansen's method is to estimate the Π matrix from an unrestricted VAR and to test whether we can reject the restrictions implied by the reduced rank of Π.

2.2.7. 3-D visualization

Visualizing information in graphical ways can give us insights into our data in order to test the validation of Tourism-led growth hypothesis. By enabling us to look at and explore data from different perspectives, visualizations help us identify patterns, connections, and relationships within the data. 3D charts display data in a 3-D coordinate system by drawing each column as a cuboid to create a 3D effect. We construct our 3

50

dimensional graphs by IBM Watson Studio. The purpose of applying this software is to verify the exported results by Eviews.

2.3. Empirical results

2.3.1. Empirical results for the first period 1980-1989

> ## Unit root test for 1980-1989

Table 5 shows the results of the **Levin, Lin and Chu test (2002)** for the time-series for GDP, international tourism arrivals and the others control variables. The null hypothesis is that the series has a unit root (non-stationary process). It can be seen from the table, that the series are stationary at first difference. We can reject the null hypothesis and suggest that data is stationary at first difference for the first period (1980-1989), indicating that all variables are integrated of order one, I (1).

Table 5. Group unit root test: Summary for the first period 1980-1989 in the first difference

Method	Statistic	Prob.	Cross-sections	Obs
Null: Unit root (assumes common unit root process)				
Levin, Lin & Chu t**	-4.02331	0.0000	6	44
Null: Unit root (assumes individual unit root process)				
Im, Pesaran and Shin W-stat	-3.94639	0.0000	6	44
ADF - Fisher Chi-square	40.8224	0.0001	6	44
PP - Fisher Chi-square	46.6085	0.0000	6	46

Source: Authors' calculations.

> **Empirical results from correlation analysis and Granger Causality Test for the period of communism (1980-1989)**

Table 6. Correlation matrix of the examined variables for the first period 1980-1989

	HDI	GDP	INFL	POP	ITA	PPP
HDI	1.000000					
GDP	-0.126373	1.000000				
INFL	0.044584	-0.892150	1.000000			
POP	-0.709810	0.662231	-0.555348	1.000000		
ITA	0.233214	-0.732716	0.741191	-0.568401	1.000000	
PPP	0.966142	0.014528	-0.104951	-0.678039	0.120001	1.000000

Source: Authors' calculations.

The results of the correlation analysis for the period of communism are showed in *Table 6.* From the correlation analysis we reveal that in the period of communism, GDP growth is influenced negatively by inflation and international tourism arrivals *(Table 6).* The strongest negative influence is the one of inflation rates (-0.892150). The influence of the tourist variables is (-0.732716). These results mean that inflation rates and international tourist arrivals are in inverse relationship, namely the increasing levels of the both- inflation and arrivals lead to decreasing levels of GDP growth. The others control variables: population growth and GDG PPP influence positively on the economic growth of Bulgaria during 1980-1989. The coefficients' values are respectively (0.6662231) and (0.014528). We should emphasize that the growth of population of Bulgaria during the explored period has strong straightforward influence on the economic growth of Bulgaria. The inflows of international tourists have positive influence over the measure of average achievement in key dimensions of human development: a long and healthy life, being knowledgeable and have a decent standard of living, measured by HDI. International tourist arrivals influence negatively on the population dynamics during the communism period. The coefficient value is (-0.568401).

From the results from Granger causality test, presented in *Table* 7 we prove bilateral relationship between inflation and GDP growth. On the other hand, the three variables for economic development of Bulgaria: GDP growth, GDP at PPP and HDI are in granger causality relationship with the growth of population.

Table 7. Granger Causality Test for 1980- 1989 (2 lags)

Null hypothesis	F-Statistic	P value	Decision
GDP does not Granger Cause HDI	0.32883	0.7428	Accept both hypotheses
HDI does not Granger Cause GDP	0.81927	0.5201	
INFL does not Granger Cause HDI	0.60414	0.6234	Accept both hypotheses
HDI does not Granger Cause INFL	1.23244	0.4479	
POP does not Granger Cause HDI	3.54613	0.1621	POP←HDI
HDI does not Granger Cause POP*	5.99197	**0.0896**	
ITA does not Granger Cause HDI	0.03510	0.9661	Accept both hypotheses
HDI does not Granger Cause ITA	0.03597	0.9653	
PPP does not Granger Cause HDI	1.27441	0.3975	Accept both hypotheses
HDI does not Granger Cause PPP	3.85847	0.1481	
INFL does not Granger Cause GDP*	28.6562	**0.0337**	INF $\rightarrow$ GDP
GDP does not Granger Cause INFL*	10.9876	**0.0834**	INF←GDP
POP does not Granger Cause GDP	5.13092	0.1076	POP←GDP
GDP does not Granger Cause POP*	7.85525	**0.0642**	
ITA does not Granger Cause GDP	0.15610	0.8650	Accept both hypotheses
GDP does not Granger Cause ITA	0.03723	0.9641	
PPP does not Granger Cause GDP	2.19358	0.2588	Accept both hypotheses
GDP does not Granger Cause PPP	0.47620	0.6613	
POP does not Granger Cause INFL	8.14729	0.1093	Accept both hypotheses
INFL does not Granger Cause POP	7.06277	0.1240	
ITA does not Granger Cause INFL	0.03980	0.9617	Accept both hypotheses
INFL does not Granger Cause ITA	0.27701	0.7831	
PPP does not Granger Cause INF	2.75041	0.2666	Accept both hypotheses
INFL does not Granger Cause PPP	0.89032	0.5290	
ITA does not Granger Cause POP	1.13923	0.4675	Accept both hypotheses
POP does not Granger Cause ITA	0.97331	0.5068	
PPP does not Granger Cause POP*	42.4133	**0.0063**	PPP $\rightarrow$ POP
POP does not Granger Cause PPP	2.29365	0.2486	
PPP does not Granger Cause ITA	0.35310	0.7390	Accept both hypotheses
ITA does not Granger Cause PPP	0.33761	0.7476	

* Null Hypothesis rejection at 10% significance level and acceptance of the Alternative Hypothesis which determine informational influence of the relevant variable
Source: Authors' calculations.

54

> ### Empirical results from the linear regression for the first period (1980-1989)

In order to reveal the direct influence of tourism sector to GDP growth, we apply linear regression *(Table 8).*

The constructed equation is significant with Significance F lower than 0.05- (0.047760206). The results are consistent with the results from the correlation analysis. The impact of international tourist arrivals is negative. The coefficient value is significant at 5% level of significance and it is equal to (-1,79932340451273E-06). Considering the linear specification, this suggests the following: if international tourist arrivals increase by one standard deviation, the GDP growth rate decrease by 17.9 %. The overall fit of the model is sufficient as supported by statistically significant F-test and the amount variance in dependent variable explained by the independent variables (R squared =0.40).

Table 8. Linear Regression analysis for the first period (1980-1989)

Regression Statistics	
Multiple R	0.636692745
R Square	0.405377651
Adjusted R Square	0.331049858
Standard Error	2.91751459
Observations	10

ANOVA	df	SS	MS	F	Significance F			
Regression	1	46.42315	46.42315	5.453917464	0.047760206			
Residual	8	68.09513	8.511891					
Total	9	114.5183						

	Coefficients	Standard Error	t Stat	P-value	Lower 95%	Upper 95%	Lower 95,0%	Upper 95,0%
Intercept	8.490857116	2.118889985	4.007219	0.00391019	3.604688049	13.37702618	3.604688049	13.37702618
ITA	-1.79932E-06	7.70469E-07	-2.33536	0.047760206	-3.57603E-06	-2.262E-08	-3.57603E-06	2.26196E-08

Source: Authors' calculations.

> ➤ **Empirical results from Johansen cointegration test for the first period (1980-1989)**

Table 9. Johansen Cointegration Test for the second period 1990-2017

Ho: No of CE(s)	Trace Test			Maximum Eigen-value		
	Trace Statistic	0.05 Critical Value	Prob.**	Max-Eigen Statistic T-critical	0.05 Critical Value	Prob.**
None *	24.14820	15.49471	0.0020	21.53253	14.26460	0.0030
At most 1	2.615665	3.841466	0.1058	2.615665	3.841466	0.1058

Source: Authors' calculations.
Trace test indicates 1 cointegrating eqn(s) at the 0.05 level
* denotes rejection of the hypothesis at the 0.05 level
**MacKinnon-Haug-Michelis (1999) p-values

We conducted a lag order selection criteria tests in order to obtain the optimal lag length for the Johansen cointegration examination. Having established that the variables are all integrated at first differences, we use four selection criterions, namely; HQ, AIC, FPE, and LR to determine the optimal lag to be used in the model. We find out that two (2) lags were suggested as the optimal lag length. Thus, two lags are used in Johansen cointegration test. Having determined that variables are integrated at first difference and the optimal lag length, it is necessary to establish whether there exists a non-spurious and stable relationship with at least a single linear combination between the regressors. Thus, we conduct the Johansen cointegration test based on the Trace statistic and Max-Eigenvalue statistics. The results from the Johansen cointegration test are presented in Table 7. Results show one cointegrating equation ($r \leq 1$) in Trace test statistic results as well as the Max-Eigenvalue revealed one co-integrating equation at 0.05 level of significance. Hence, the null hypothesis of no cointegrating equation (r=0) is rejected. Consequently, variables are cointegrated, simply implying that there exists a long-run relationship within the series.

2.3.2. Empirical results for the second period 1990 - 2017

> **Unit root test for the second period (1990-2017)**

Table 10. Group unit root test: Summary for the second period 1990-2017

Method	Statistic	Prob.	Cross-sections	Obs
Null: Unit root (assumes common unit root process)				
Levin, Lin & Chu t**	-10.7309	0.0000	6	154
Null: Unit root (assumes individual unit root process)				
Im, Pesaran and Shin W-stat	-10.7026	0.0000	6	154
ADF - Fisher Chi-square	105.446	0.0000	6	154
PP - Fisher Chi-square	123.449	0.0000	6	156

Source: Authors' calculations.

Again, group unit root test is applied to examine the stationary properties of the time series for the second period 1990-2017 *(Table 10).* The results show that the null hypothesis of the existence of unit root cannot be rejected for GDP, international tourism arrivals (ITA) and the others control variables at level, thus implying the non-stationarity of all variables. However, the null hypothesis of unit root is rejected for the first order difference of GDP, ITA and the

58

others control variables, and this confirms the stationarity of all variables at the first differences, indicating that all variables are integrated of order one, I (1).

➤ **Empirical results from correlation analysis and Granger Causality Test for the second period (1990-2017)**

Table 11. Correlation matrix of the examined variables for the second period 1990-2017

	HDI	GDP	INFL	ITA	POP	PPP
HDI	1.000000					
GDP	0.400871	1.000000				
INFL	-0.354281	-0.230849	1.000000			
ITA	0.924619	0.181326	-0.304183	1.000000		
POP	0.215160	0.116770	0.090853	0.218853	1.000000	
PPP	0.986609	0.335667	-0.304368	0.938540	0.253672	1.000000

Source: Authors' calculations.

From the results of correlation test for 1990-2017, presented in *Table 11* we should emphasize that international tourist arrivals influence positively on the GDP growth. The coefficient value is equal to (0.181326) which is weaker than the same one in the communism period (-0.7327160). Inflation is the variable that keeps its negative influence (-0.230849) but we should mention that this relation is not as strong as the one in the previous time period. Another transformation of the relationship from negative to positive is the connection between the dynamics of tourists' inflows and population growth. The coefficient value is equal to (0.218853). This may be explained by the change of fiscal politics and joining to the

European Union during 2007. International tourist arrivals have strong straightforward relationship with HDI of Bulgaria with a weight of the coefficient (0.924619). From the results above, we may conclude that the more integrated the Bulgarian market is, the more attractive for tourists is. ITA impacts negatively on the inflation rates. It contradicts to the results for the communism period. Tourist sector influence GDP growth indirectly by determining inflation rates. The coefficient is equal to (-0.304183). Comparing the weights of the coefficients, we observe transformation of the influence- from strong and positive to medium and negative.

Table 12 shows the results of Granger causality test for the post-communism period. Here, we should mark the existence of more significant causalities in the post-communism period than the same during communism. Population growth granger causes the HDI of Bulgaria. HDI growth and GDG at PPP granger cause ITA. These results confirm the ones from the correlation analysis, namely the economic development determines the wish of tourists to visit Bulgaria. Tourists' inflows determine inflation levels. On the other side according to correlation analysis and granger results, inflation is in negative granger relation with GDP growth.

Table 12. Granger Causality Test for the second period 1990-2017 (2 lags)

Null hypothesis	F-Statistic	P value	Decision
GDP does not Granger Cause HDI	1.84340	0.1830	Accept both hypotheses
HDI does not Granger Cause GDP	0.22068	0.8038	
INFL does not Granger Cause HDI	0.38122	0.6877	Accept both hypotheses
HDI does not Granger Cause INFL	1.40890	0.2666	
POP does not Granger Cause HDI*	2.65481	**0.0938**	POP $\rightarrow$ HDI
HDI does not Granger Cause POP	0.32814	0.7239	
ITA does not Granger Cause HDI	2.19296	0.1365	HDI $\rightarrow$ ITA
HDI does not Granger Cause ITA*	8.97929	**0.0015**	
PPP does not Granger Cause HDI	0.19522	0.8241	HDI $\rightarrow$ PPP
HDI does not Granger Cause PPP*	5.34847	**0.0133**	
INFL does not Granger Cause GDP*	3.86965	**0.0371**	INF $\rightarrow$ GDP
GDP does not Granger Cause INFL	0.13888	0.8711	
POP does not Granger Cause GDP	0.17958	0.8369	Accept both hypotheses
GDP does not Granger Cause POP	1.22796	0.3131	
ITA does not Granger Cause GDP	1.42317	0.2633	Accept both hypotheses
GDP does not Granger Cause ITA	0.85175	0.4409	
PPP does not Granger Cause GDP	2.19358	0.2588	Accept both hypotheses
GDP does not Granger Cause PPP	0.47620	0.6613	
POP does not Granger Cause INFL	0.31448	0.7335	Accept both hypotheses
INFL does not Granger Cause POP	0.25764	0.7753	
ITA does not Granger Cause INFL*	3.64016	**0.0439**	ITA $\rightarrow$ INF
INFL does not Granger Cause ITA	1.90717	0.1734	
PPP does not Granger Cause INFL	0.89984	0.4217	Accept both hypotheses
INFL does not Granger Cause PPP	1.83115	0.1849	
ITA does not Granger Cause POP	1.73481	0.2008	Accept both hypotheses
POP does not Granger Cause ITA	1.25239	0.3063	
PPP does not Granger Cause POP	0.51355	0.6057	Accept both hypotheses
POP does not Granger Cause PPP	0.17928	0.8371	
PPP does not Granger Cause ITA*	3.70086	**0.0420**	PPP $\rightarrow$ ITA
ITA does not Granger Cause PPP	0.23498	0.7926	

* Null Hypothesis rejection at 10% significance level and acceptance of the Alternative Hypothesis which determine informational influence of the relevant variable
Source: Authors' calculations.

A comparison between both explored periods is exposed by *Graph 1.* We should mark that reversing of the significant relations is observed. During communism, the economic development of Bulgaria determines the growth of population and GDP is influenced only by the inflation levels. Tourism sector is not a significant factor for the Bulgarian economy during this period. Before 1990 Bulgaria was not totally deprived of international tourist arrivals but neither was it actively involved in them.

During the period of 1990-2017, we reveal active interactions between the explored variables. The relationship between GDP growth and tourism provides valuable information on how to program tourism activity from private investors. In particular, given the simultaneous links between growth and tourism, forecasts of general growth in the economy are signals that can help in the timing of supply-side services in tourism organizations. Changes in international tourist arrivals impact other sectors and variables (inflation rates) and by this it produces multiplier effect of tourism. The magnitude of tourism multiplier depends on the country's size of territory and self-sufficiency of productivity. These conclusions of our analysis can be useful to policy makers, investors and business sector. They may be encouraged to devise sectoral policies able to support Bulgarian destinations since there are significant returns for the economy in terms of higher GDP growth rates and lowering the inflation rates. In line with intuition and extant empirical evidence inflation, rate and population growth rate are related to economic growth. As suggested by Bittencourt (2012 p. 334) "high inflation is detrimental to growth …[I]t either outweighs the Mundell–Tobin effect, or creates particular distortions, including increased volatility and uncertainty, which results in a shift to less productive activities and consequently slower growth rates".

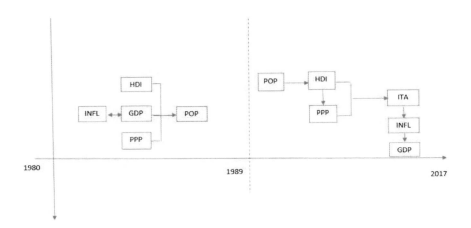

Graph 1
Results from Granger Causality Test for both explored periods

In order to visualize a relation between economic activity and tourism industry, we apply 3D cubic visualization. By Graph 2 we reveal the relation between inflation, GDP and international tourist arrivals. It is proved that the relationship between tourism and economic activity (GDP and inflation) is very weak and for most of the values it is missing. These results confirm the ones by correlation analysis and Granger causality test. We may conclude that the tourism-led growth hypothesis is rejected during the communism period in Bulgaria.

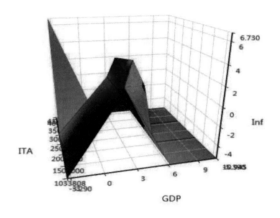

Graph 2

3- D visualization of relationship between economic activity and tourism for the first period (1980-1989)

In order to compare the dynamic of the relationship between communism and post-communism period, we have constructed a 3D visualization for the second period 1990-2017 (Graph 3). We confirm that the relationship between economic activity and tourism industry is sustainable for the whole period of time. It exists a maximum value in their relation. This may be explained by the financial crisis during

2007-2008 when the development of the tourism industry is a key factor for managing the negative subsequence from the financial distress. The results by Graph 3 confirm the Tourism-led Growth Hypothesis for the second period (1990-2017).

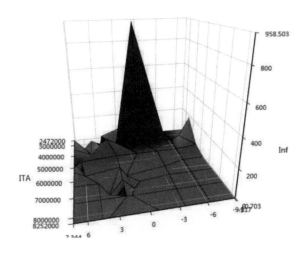

Graph 3

3- D visualization of relationship between economic activity and tourism for the second period (1990-2017)

➢ **Empirical results from the linear regression for the second period (1990-2017)**

Table 13. Linear Regression analysis for the second period (1990-2017)

Regression Statistics	
Multiple R	0.18132645
R Square	0.03287928
Adjusted R Square	-0.00431767
Standard Error	4.72378228
Observations	28

ANOVA

	df	SS	MS	F	Significance F
Regression	1	19.72399	19.72399	0.883924	0.00578256
Residual	26	580.1671	22.31412		
Total	27	599.8911			

	Coefficients	Standard Error	t Stat	P-value	Lower 95%	Upper 95%	Lower 95,0%	Upper 95,0%
Intercept	0.98741367	2.793350796	2.353487	0.026573	-6.72922846	4.75440113	-6.72922846	4.754401129
ITA	5.1685E-07	5.49738E-07	2.940172	0.005783	-6.13154E-07	1.6469E-06	-6.1315E-07	1.64685E-06

Source: Authors' calculations.

In order to reveal the direct influence of tourism sector to GDP growth, we apply linear regression *(Table 13)*. The constructed equation is significant with Significance F lower than 0.05- (0.005783). The results are consistent with the results from the correlation analysis, either. The impact of international tourist arrivals is positive. The coefficient value is significant at 5% level of significance and it is equal to (5.5E-07). Considering the linear specification, this suggests the following: if international tourist arrivals increase by one standard deviation, the GDP growth rate increase by 5.51.7% .The overall fit of the model is sufficient as supported by statistically significant F-test and the amount variance in dependent variable explained by the independent variables (R squared =0.03). From the linear regression results, we find an evidence for confirming the ones of correlation analysis and granger causality test. We observe converse influence again-from negative to positive. Tourism spillovers may be used to impoverished households and increase earnings and they could become a large-scale resource transfer tool, able to alleviate poverty levels and increase final consumption.

> **Empirical results from Johansen cointegration test for the second period (1990-2017)**

Table 13. Johansen Cointegration Test for the second
period 1990-2017

Ho: No of	Trace Test			Maximum Eigen-value		
CE(s)	Trace Statistic	0.05 Critical Value	Prob.**	Max-Eigen Statistic T-critical	0.05 Critical Value	Prob.**
None *	16.93878	15.49471	0.0301	16.93836	14.26460	0.0184
At most 1	0.000421	3.841466	0.9855	0.000421	3.841466	0.9855

Source: Authors' calculations.
Trace test indicates 1 cointegrating eqn(s) at the 0.05 level
* denotes rejection of the hypothesis at the 0.05 level
**MacKinnon-Haug-Michelis (1999) p-values

Again, we conduct a lag order selection criteria tests in order to obtain the optimal lag length for the Johansen cointegration examination. Having established that the variables are all integrated at first differences, we use four selection criterions, namely; HQ, AIC, FPE, and LR to determine the optimal lag to be used in the model. Thus, two (2) lags were suggested as the optimal lag length and also two lags are used in Johansen cointegration test. Having determined that variables are integrated at first difference and the optimal lag length, we have to find whether there exists a non-spurious and stable relationship with at least a single linear combination between the regressors. Consequently, we apply the Johansen cointegration test based on the Trace statistic and Max-Eigenvalue statistics. The results from the Johansen cointegration test are shown in *Table 14.* Results indicate one cointegrating equation (r≤1) in Trace test statistic results as well as the Max-Eigenvalue revealed one co-integrating equation at 0.05 level of significance. Therefore, the null hypothesis of no cointegrating equation (r=0) is rejected. Consequently, variables are cointegrated, simply implying that there exists a long-run relationship within the series.

https://doi.org/10.2478/9788395793806-004

CONCLUSION

The aim of this research is to explore the relationship between tourism and economic development of Bulgaria in the period of communism and the one of post-communism. In this study we intend to elaborate the history of the Bulgarian tourism industry trends from the Communism to its contemporary policy making. We make attempts to investigate the validity of the tourism-led-growth (TLG) hypotheses in Bulgaria. Our dataset contains annual observations at a country level over the years 1980-2017. The explored time period is divided into two sub-periods: 1980-1989- a period when communism is established; 1990-2017- a post-communism period. Data applied for Bulgaria are annual time series but we experienced limitations and our research was restricted by restrained axes to data for the Communism and pre-Communism periods. We prove that during communism, the economic development of Bulgaria determines the growth of population and GDP is influenced only by the inflation levels. Tourism sector is not a significant factor for the Bulgarian economy during this period. Before 1990 Bulgaria was not totally deprived of international tourist arrivals but neither was it actively involved in them. During the period of 1990-2017, we reveal active interactions between the explored variables.

Furthermore, **Stoilova (2013)** prove that the tourism has contributed to improvement of the main economic indicators and therefore is considered as essential development generator for the period 1998-2013. She established that at the same time, tourism in Bulgaria is facing serious structural weaknesses, namely one-sided product mix, dependence on limited number of markets, high seasonality, low performance indicators, and extreme territorial concentration limiting the wider spread of its benefits, while significant part of tourism potential remains unexploited. Our findings reconfirm the analysis made by **Stoilova (2013).**

The relationship between GDP growth and tourism provides valuable information on how to program tourism activity from private investors. In particular, given the simultaneous links between growth and tourism, forecasts of general growth in the economy are signals that can help in the timing of supply-side services in tourism organizations. Changes in international tourist arrivals impact other sectors and variables (inflation rates) and by this it produces multiplier effect of tourism. The magnitude of tourism multiplier depends on the country's size of territory and self-sufficiency of productivity. These conclusions of our analysis can be useful to policy makers, investors and business sector. They may be encouraged to devise sectoral policies able to support

71

Bulgarian destinations since there are significant returns for the economy in terms of higher GDP growth rates and lowering the inflation rates. In line with intuition and extant empirical evidence inflation, rate and population growth rate are related to economic growth. Moreover, we prove that tourism has mattered in the economic growth process of Bulgaria in the last 19 years.

We intend a future research direction towards explore the relationship between tourism growth and exchange rate in Bulgaria for the economy transition period.

REFERENCES

Aslan, A. (2013), Tourism development and economic growth in the Mediterranean countries: Evidence from panel Granger causality tests. *Current Issues in Tourism,* 17(4), 363-372.

Balaguer, J., & Cantavella-Jordá, M. (2002). Tourism as a long-run economic growth factor: the Spanish case. *Applied Economics,* 34, 877-884.

Bento, J. (2016). Tourism and economic growth in Portugal: an empirical investigation of causal links. *Tourism & Management Studies,* 12(1), 164-171. https://dx.doi.org/10.18089/tms.2016.12117.

Bittencourt, M. (2012). Inflation and Economic Growth in Latin America: Some Panel Time-Series Evidence. University of Pretoria, Department of Economics, *Working Papers.* 29.

Brida J., Cortes-Jimenez I., & Pulina M. (2014). Has the tourism-led growth hypothesis been validated? A literature review, *Current Issues in Tourism,* 19 (5), 394-430, DOI: 10.1080/13683500.2013.868414.

Brida, J., Sánchez, E., & Risso, W. (2008). Tourism's impact on long-run Mexican economic growth. *Economics Bulletin,* 3, 1-8.

Chen, C., & Chiou-Wei, S. (2009). Tourism expansion, tourism uncertainty and economic growth: new evidence from Taiwan and Korea. *Tourism Management,* 30, 812–818.

Chou M. C. (2013). Does tourism development promote economic growth in transition countries? A panel data analysis. *Economic Modelling,* 33, 226-232.

Coşkun, I. & Özer, M. (2014). A Reexamination of the Tourism-Led Growth Hypothesis under growth and tourism uncertainties in Turkey. European Journal of Business and Social Sciences, Vol.3, No 8,pp. 256-272

Demirhan, B. (2016). Tourism-Led Growth Hypothesis in Mediterranean Countries: Evidence from a Panale cointegration and and error Correction Model, *Applied Economics and Finance, 3, pp. 38- 53.* https://pdfs.semanticscholar.org/ebdd/8aa99b1b756ac69e45c 6e39d15deffb32f30.pdf

Deng, T. & Ma, M. (2014). Resource curse in tourism economies? An investigation of China's world cultural and natural heritage sites. *Asia Pacific Journal of Tourism Research,* 19, 809-822.

Deng, T., Ma, M., & Cao, J. (2014). Tourism resource development and long term economic growth: a resource curse hypothesis approach. *Tourism Economics,* 20, 923–938.

Dimitrov P., Kraseta, R., Dimitrov B., & Parvanov, P. (2018). Bulgarian tourism and the problem of poverty in Bulgaria. *Tourism & Management Studies*, 14 (2), 45-52.

Engle, R., & Granger, C. (1987). Cointegration and Error Correction: Representation, Estimation and Testing. *Econometrica*, 55, 251-276. http://dx.doi.org/10.2307/1913236.

Granger, C. W. J. (1969). Investigating Causal Relations by Econometric Models and Cross-Spectral Methods. *Econometrica*, 37, 424-438.

Gunduz, L., & Hatemi-J, A. (2005). Is the Tourism-led Growth Hypothesis Valid for Turkey?. *Applied Economics Letters*, 12, 499-504.

Harrison, D. (1993). Bulgarian tourism: A state of uncertainty. Annals of Tourism Research, 20(3), Pages 519-534. doi: https://doi.org/10.1016/0160-7383 (93)90007-P

Holzner, M. (2011). Tourism and economic development: The beach disease? *Tourism Management*, 32, 922-933.

Ivanov, S. (2017). Mass tourism in Bulgaria: The Force awakens. In R. S. David Harrison, Mass tourism in a small world. *UK: Wallingford: CABI.* 168-180. doi: DOI: 10.1079/9781780648545.0168

Johansen, S. (1991). Estimation and Hypothesis Testing of Cointegration Vectors in Gaussian Vector Autoregressive Models. *Econometrica,* 59 (6), 1551–1580.

Johansen, S. (1995). Likelihood-Based Inference in Cointegrated Vector Autoregressive Models. *New York: Oxford University Press.*

Kiryakova-Dineva, T., Kyurova, V. & Chankova, Y. (2019). Soft skills for sustainable development in tourism: the Bulgarian experience. *European Journal of Sustainable Development*, 8 (2), 57-68.

Lee, C. G. (2012). Tourism, trade, and income: evidence from Singapore. *Anatolia: An International Journal of Tourism and Hospitality Research,* 23 (3), 348–358.

Lee, C., & Chang, C. (2008). Tourism development and economic growth: A closer look at panels. *Tourism Management,* 29(1), 180-192.

Levin, A., Chien-Fu, L., & Chia-Shang, J. Ch. (2002). Unit root tests in panel data: asymptotic and finite-sample properties. *Journal of Econometrics, Elsevier,* 108(1), 1-24.

Meyer, D. F. (2018). An Analysis of the Impact of Economic Growth, Political Instability and Exchange Rate on Tourism Growth in South Africa, Working papers 04DM, *Research Association for Interdisciplinary Studies.*

Nowak, J.-J., & Sahli, P. (2007). Coastal tourism and "Dutch disease" in a small island economy. *Tourism Economics,* 13, 49-65.

Oh, C. K. (2005). The contribution of tourism development to economic growth in the Korean economy. *Tourism Management,* 26, 39–44.

Payne, J. E., & Mervar, A. (2010). The tourism–growth nexus in Croatia. *Tourism Economics,* 16, 1089–1094.

Ridderstaat, J., Croes, R., & Nijkamp, P. (2013). Modeling Tourism Development and Long-Run Economic Growth in Aruba. *Tinbergen Institute Discussion Paper* 13-145/VIII. Available at SSRN: https://ssrn.com/abstract=2328127.

Salahodjaev, R., & Safarova, N. (2015). Do foreign visitors reward post-communist countries? A panel evidence for tourism-growth nexus, *MPRA Paper 66215,* University Library of Munich, Germany.

Sapundzhi F., Dzimbova T., Pencheva N., & Milanov P. (2016). Comparative evaluation of four scoring functions with three models of delta opioid receptor using molecular docking. *Der Pharma Chemica,* 8 (11), 118-124, ISSN 0975-413X.

Shahzad, S. J. H., Muhammad, S., Román F., & Ravinesh, K. R. (2016). Tourism-led Growth Hypothesis in the Top Ten Tourist Destinations: New Evidence Using the Quantile-on-

Quantile Approach. *MPRA Paper,* Available at: https://mpra.ub.uni-muenchen.de/75540/.

Shan, J., & Wilson K. (2001). Causality between trade and tourism: empirical evidence from China. *Applied Economics Letters,* 8, 279-283.

Singh, D. R. (2008). Small island developing states (SIDS). *Tourism and economic development. Tourism Analysis,* 13, 629–636.

Stoilova, D. (2013). Tourism industry and economic development in Bulgaria. Romanian Economic and Business Review, 8 (4.1), 60-68.

Suhel, S., & Bashir, A. (2018). The role of tourism toward economic growth in the local economy. *Economic Journal of Emerging Markets,* 10, 32-39.

Suresh, J., & Senthilnathan, S. (2014). Relationship between Tourism and Economic Growth in Sri Lanka. *SSRN Electronic Journal.* http://ssrn.com/abstract=2373931.

Surugiu, C., & Surugiu, M. R. (2013). Is the tourism sector supportive of economic growth? Empirical evidence on Romanian tourism. *Tourism Economics,* 19(1), 115–132.

Tang, C. F., & Tan, E. C. (2015). Does tourism effectively stimulate Malaysia's economic growth? *Tourism Management,* 46, 158-163.

Tang, C. H., & Jang, S. (2009). The tourism-economy causality in the United States: A subindustry level examination. *Tourism Management,* 30, 553-558.

Tang, C.F., & Abosedra, S. (2016). Tourism and growth in Lebanon: new evidence from bootstrap simulation and rolling causality approaches. *Empirical Economics,* 50, 679-696.

Traykov, M., Trencheva, M., Stavrova, E., Mavrevski, R., & Trenchev, I. (2018). Risk analysis in the economics through R Language, *WSEAS transactions on business and economics,* 15, 180-186. http://www.wseas.org/multimedia/journals/economics/2018/a 365907-603.pdf.

Иванов, Д. (2014). Пазарът. In Д. Иванов, От Девети до Десети (р. 830). София.: Захарий Стоянов, УИ "Св.Климент Охридски". doi: 9540720184

Иванова, М. (2018). Туризъм под надзор. Балкантурист - началото на международния и масов туризъм в България. София: Сиела.

Маринова, К. (30 04 2017 г.). Вестник "Труд". Извлечено от Клемент Готвалд докарал чехкините у нас на море: https://trud.bg/%D0%BA%D0%BB%D0%B5%D0%BC%D0 %B5%D0%BD%D1%82- %D0%B3%D0%BE%D1%82%D0%B2%D0%B0%D0%BB %D0%B4-

%D0%B4%D0%BE%D0%BA%D0%B0%D1%80%D0%B0%D0%BB-%D1%87%D0%B5%D1%85%D0%BA%D0%B8%D0%BD%D0%B8%D1%82%D0%B5-%D0%BD%D0%B0/

Йорданов, Й., & Алексова, Д. (2013). Насоки за устойчиво развитие на здравния туризъм в България. Управление и устойчиво развитие, (р. 106). Юндола.

Appendix 1.

The dynamics of the variables for the first period (1980-1989)

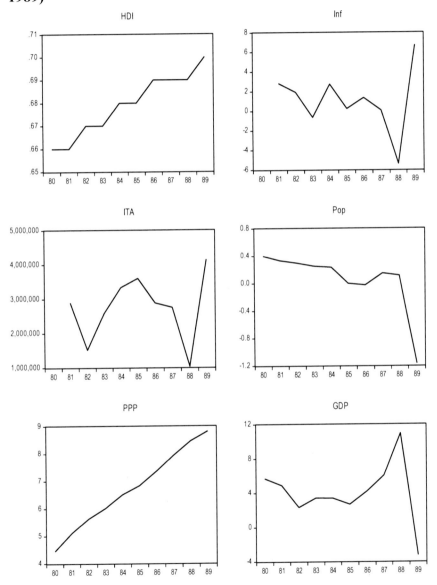

Appendix 2.

The dynamics of the variables for the second period (1990-2017)

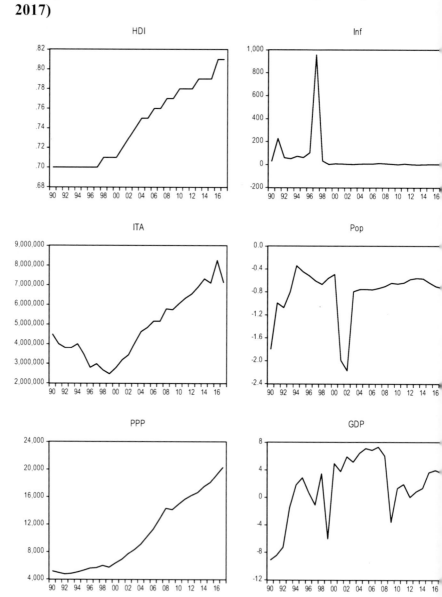